Step Into New Earth:
Moving Beyond the Glitch

Spells, Odes & Codes

Cheryl Lunar Wind & Friends

Step Into New Earth: Moving Beyond the Glitch
Spells, Odes & Codes

Copyright © 2025 by Cheryl Lunar Wind

Cheryl's poetry in this collection may be shared, or printed with credit given to the author. All other contributors keep rights to their work.

Any Inquiries contact:

cheryl.hiller@yahoo.com

Some of the poems in this collection first appeared in Star Messages and Crossroads of Change chapbooks; Lemurian Revival, College of the Siskiyous and on facebook.

Front cover photo credit to Maggie Enoch

Back cover credit to Jennifer Hershelman

First edition.

Published by Alexander Agency Books,
Mount Shasta, California 96067

ISBN 979-8-9927622-0-4

Step Into New Earth:
Moving Beyond the Glitch

Spells, Odes & Codes

Preface

Below are some gems found in this volume. Look inside to find more.

"Did you get the message that the Golden Age is finally here?"
--Shivrael p. 19

"You are -- Intuitive, Resilient, Sovereign."
--Dave and Starfish p.54

"The Regreening of your inner world is the most important work you have in the world, for the world, at this time."
--Sabina and Herd of Light p.48

"Barren boats cactus throats
Sighs walk where desert goes."
--Kazi p.15

"Ride the wheel
Cycles upon cycles."
--Shivrael p.38

"There is no right or wrong,
only needs met or unmet."
--Cody p.50

"What if ideas were hunters?"
--Benjamin p.58

"All you need to do now is trust, listen and dare
to play your song."
--Mikasa p.55

"Universal Knowledge, Telepathy, Clairvoyance and so many more godly gifts will be granted."
--Vivian p.46,47

"Your meant to wear a crown."
--Danielle p.8

Contents

The State of Denmark 1
by Rune Darling

The Glitch 2
by Mikasa Tamara Blue Ray

Breaking the Spell 2
by Cheryl

Zero Point 3
by Mikasa Tamara Blue Ray

All That We Are 4
by Kazi Ayaz Mahesar

All I Am 5
by Mercy Talley

Ma'at Really Matters 6, 7
by Vivian Marie McIntosh

The World's A Stage 8, 9
by Danielle Turner

We Are the Seeds 10, 11
by Cody Ray Richardson

A Cuckoo in Her Nest 12
by Cheryl

The Store by Cheryl 13

Lips of Drought 14, 15
by Kazi Ayaz Mahesar

No More So Dry 15
by Kazi Ayaz Mahesar

Liberation by Zin Onyx 16

GO IN PEACE 17
by A'Marie B. Thomas-Brown

Transmutation by Shivrael 18, 19

Arrival by Shivrael 19

Sunlight by Aria Squire 20

You Have Other Streams 21
by Kazi Ayaz Mahesar

Be Here Now by Shivrael 22

Knickerbocker glory 23
by Daniel Stone

Being Human 24
by Cody Ray Richardson

Every Once in a While 25
by Cheryl

Broken Families 26, 27
by Cheryl

Rainbow Warrior 28, 29
by Shivrael

Reflection by Cheryl 29
(Step Into New Earth)

Freedom 30
by Cody Ray Richardson

To Fly Once More 31
by Cody Ray Richardson

For the Love of We 32
by Shivrael

I AM : WE ARE 33
by Cheryl

The finite is the moment's gift 34, 35
by Cody Ray Richardson

Transformation 35
by Pradeep Nawarathna

Coffee by Dan Crusey 36

Seeking by Dan Crusey 37

The Wheel 38, 39
by Shivrael

Over and over and over again 40, 41
by Cody Ray Richardson

Ode to Isis Sophia Maria Magdalena 42, 43
by Mikasa Tamara Blue Ray

Dance 44, 45
by Jennifer Hershelman

Blossoming Time 46
by Shivrael

When Your Ascending 47
by Alex Hogstrum

Seraphic Sibyl's Sweven 48, 49
by Vivian Marie McIntosh

Regreening 50, 51
by Sabina and Herd of Light

Mosaic of Light 51
by Mikasa Tamara Blue Ray

What'ya Gonna Do About It 52
by Cody Ray Richardson

Hour Glass 53
by Cody Ray Richardson

KALEIDOSCOPE 54, 55
by Tommy Allen

Starfish Message 56
Goat's Message by Dave Harvey

Permission 57
by Mikasa Tamara Blue Ray

Hunters 58, 59
by Benjamin Prasad

Personality 60
by Benjamin Prasad

Worthy 61
by Jennifer Hershelman

Standing in my Sovereignty 62
by Jennifer Hershelman

Heart Beat True, 63
Perfectly Imperfect Art
by Pradeep Nawarathna

We Are Returning 64, 65
by Rune Darling

The End Game 66
by Rune Darling

Contributors page
Author page

The State of Denmark
by Rune Darling

Something Is Out Of Tune
In The State Of Denmark
.
So This Night I Am Going To
Leave This World Behind
.
To Rearrange The Cosmic Alphabet
So Mannaz & Berkana Can Be Together
.
No More Loki Shall Reside Within
Expelled By A Mighty Spell I Cast
.
.
By The Wings of Azrael
Guardian at The Veil Between
.
I Summon Now The Light
That Through The Shadows Weaves
.
From Dust to Stars Where Ancient Echoes Call
Through This spell I Command The Barriers to Fall
.
My Love Binds The Bridge of Night to Day
Light The Paths where The Lost Find their Way
.
With This Chant I Weave Protection Far and Wide
Let None but Peace Upon these Sacred Winds Now Ride
.
In My Grace Through Realms of Time and Space
Pass Safely Spirits of The Transient World
.
.

The Glitch
by Mikasa Tamara Blue Ray

So let us begin
With new eyes the world will be seen
Remember your origin
Don't mind the holographic screen
Spiritual hygiene
Best preventive medicine
And the hearts will all open wide
In such joyous pride
Walking side by side
Together so strong
Singing our power song
Such loving concert
Removing all inserts
Our reality will improve
When our thoughts no longer gloom
Just like Neo
Each one of us a brave Leo
No more separatrix
Bye bye Matrix

Breaking the Spell-

singing our power song

Opens the door--
to a new era.

We are the system busters.
(Neo led the way)

---Cheryl

Zero Point
by Mikasa Tamara Blue Ray

Zero, zero, zero, zero.

We are the Divine Hero.
Making the Shift so Clear.
Because we Are for Real.
Working for the vibrations to rise.
Even if some of us work in disguise.
A convergence of frequencies, a sweet anoint.
This yet another quantum field zero point.
Divine rays of creation.
Helping us in our Actualization.
New Earth frequencies descend.
A harmony of love, our spirits transcend.
In this quantum dance, we break old ties.
Embrace the unknown, where divinity lies.
Expanding our consciousness, from zero point we soar.

Exploring More.

With each shift and reset, we evolve.
A song of hearts, a celestial solve.

All That We Are
by Kazi Ayaz Mahesar

Deeper than I
Deeper than you

The soul
Permeates us all

All that we are
Yesterday, today, tomorrow

Beyond days and years
Beyond suns and moons

Our endless journeys
Like a witchcraft

Witched within
Bewitched bedouins

Our caravans
Into the depths of sand dunes

Strewn in our heart
Far and wide within our arms

Into the folds of all unfolding
Of the earth itself

The Earth
Like one large blue seed

Fallen from the eyes of the Creator
Condensed within

Flying flames
Brightened ambers

Forever fluorescent
Clandestine crimson blue

Deeper than I
Deeper than you

All I Am
by Mercy Talley

All that I Am written on
a paper in my pocket
to remind my heart

I'm not what the
controllers want me to be...

Scribed in a code with
sound & symbols
to be seen
when listening to
my eyes
revealing choices
gleaned that make--

One wise instead of
becoming hypnotized ~

*Ma'at Really Matters
by Vivian Marie McIntosh

Who's the one with a master plan?
Making moves in this Age of Man?

If ya dunno, now yanno!
It's the realist reality show!

We're ALL out here playing Harry Potter
World Stage Party & The Roofs On Fire

Acting out The Order of the Phoenix
Burning that mind enslaving Matrix

Bring on The Rain, we definitely need the water
Stop fake news from leading sheep to slaughter

It's gonna have to get a lot crazier though
Some sleepers are waking up real slow

Everything is going to happen exactly as needed
The New Garden of Eden will surely be weeded

Anyone not of an open heart and an open mind
That enchanted forest they are unable to find

Just like the door to The Room of Requirement
It will appear when one's heart power is vibrant

The Wayshowers will shine light on the path
Looking like Venus stepping up outta the bath

Won't miss the reflection of these shining one's trail
Sipping from the fountain of youth in their holy grail

Ego, envy and evilness will never enter the Holy Land
Only helpful hearts reaching back with a loving hand

No more people pretending to be pretty or to have any power over others Yanno like Umbridge did dressed up in pink?
My most favorite of colors!

There's a not so secret society of celestial beings
Working their magic up in the spiritual meetings

It's an Open Order, anyone can join
If they know both sides of the coin

To activate your own Threefold Flame
And earn a crown in this Earthly Game

Do the next thing that's Right
Choose to love and not to fight

Create harmony for ALL to coexist
Live in Ma'at while riding this shift

Ma'at is the Egyptian goddess of truth, justice, balance and order.

Tawnya Zeytinoglu has created a safe and sacred space to connect with others who want to learn how to make their heart as light as a feather and master the art of bringing order to chaos.
Her website is maatmatters.com.

The World's A Stage
by Danielle Turner

I was called and criticised
for calling out deception,
because people cant see
past their own perception.
People I had known my whole life
Were out here calling crazy,
But what I was doing
took so much bravery.
My soul was built
to challenge the system,
To go against the grain
To come to my own decision.
I took the time to search,
to find the truth,
I shared it bravely
and I backed it with proof.
But the fear in people's minds
were blinding their eye,
cognitive dissonance is hard to override.
But now the tides have shifted,
In waves the deception has lifted,
the darkness is revealed,
Illuminating what was once concealed.
They want you to bleed,
They siphon your loosh
on you they feed,
Leaving you in survival
So you're begging them to lead.
Every structure and system
was created to steal your wisdom,
To keep you down,
To stop you remembering
Your meant to wear a crown.
They hijack your humanity
By replacing it with vanity,
They want to strip away the god inside,
by merging you with Ai.
Now the darkness no longer hides,
its bleeding into everybody's lives,

It's a way for humanity to open their eye,
to get uncomfortable
and start reshape their lives.
We're being called to step out of the illusion,
To wake up and let go of confusion.
People are starting to see
Conspiracy theorists aren't so crazy.
The lies and deception run deep
and it's all happened right under our feet,
but we agreed we took a decree,
a birth certificate that states
we're no longer free.
But don't listen to me, what do I know?

I'm just over here watching the show.

We Are the Seeds
by Cody Ray Richardson

If I had they'd say I couldn't
If I could they'd say I shouldn't
If I did they'd say I didn't
If I didn't they'd say I wouldn't
If I wouldn't they'd say I had
Until I was driven mad
Then they'd say I was bad
I'd say no I'm not I'm mad
They'd say you can't be angry
If you are you are in trouble
It's illegal to express emotions
Unless you are them
They are the controllers
Of something that should not be controlled
Divinely guided sovereign is my soul
Still they punish me
For being free
Smash and push me into boxes
Putting the blame on me
For what others have done to them in the past
They put me in trial
Proclaiming themselves gods
Everyone else small
Then say I need to take accountability
Because I manifested all
Confused in my innocence
I meditate to stay calm
Unraveling this conundrum
Trying to sort through it all
Loads of information
Thrown at me constantly
To live is a sin
To die I will be free
Heaven is not here they say
You must act a certain way to get there
Still I see it all around
Even in their fear
I see it in the clouds
I hear it in the water

I sense it in my heart
I choke down the hard pill to swallow
I eat the poisoned food
And breathe infected air
You can not run to heaven
Heaven is everywhere
It is a place we never leave
So here we must stay and grow
For we are the seeds
In our hearts we know

A Cuckoo In Her Nest
by Cheryl

Looking for a cuckoo in the nest-
Am I she? Is it me?

Is my face too private?
Do I hide in my nest?

Will I come out again, or
have I forgotten?

Will I return to the ark, or
fly on?

Will I run out of words, smiles and
comforts for others?
Content to hide in my nest.

Just a cuckoo in her nest.

The Store
by Cheryl

Big Blue Banner with Yellow Smiley Faces

Homeless holding signs--
Need Gas or Food

Steam coming off hot pavement.

Lines painted in parallel--
marking safe zones to put your car.

Tall metal poles
with square light boxes on top.

Seagulls crying, wandering
the paved ground.

Token trees in little triangles.

Dogs barking--
left in parked vehicles.

Huge building--
people of all ages entering.

The sliding glass doors
opening and closing.

Other people leaving
pushing loaded carts.

Loud speakers announcing
the latest COVID precautions.

On your way out,
a smiling senior asks--

Did you find what you need?

Lips of Drought
by Kazi Ayaz Mahesar

Chameleons have sent you letters
Lip sealed words of lizards

Warning you
Of Bronze-Age skies

Of the terror of tornadoes
Of the Venus volcanoes

Earthly earthquakes
Rumbling towards you

Peaks falling in valleys
Valleys into oceans

Rings of flagrant fire
Burning fragrances

Oaks and Red-Forest trees
Dusty winds fiery breeze

Soiled into their stumps
Coiled by coal-eating serpents

Singing crying, crying singing
Wringing in your ears

Blinding you in your eyes
Hills flying as cotton flies

And you refused to read
The letters by chameleons

You refused to see
The lips of drought

Fiercely billowing blizzards
Lip sealed words of lizards

Dried lakes empty vessels
Earthy earthlings

Barren boats cactus throats
Sighs walk where desert goes

Silent loud
Lips of drought

Eyes of river
Thirst of cloud

No More So Dry
by Kazi Ayaz Mahesar

Whenever you think
You should come

You may in your love
Remember God knows

What you hide
So, come closer

To your soul
To your heart

So, drop
In the ocean

That is Us
That is Bliss

No more the sky
No more so dry

No more the earth
Just us

This moment
This breath

Liberation
by Zin Onyx

Out with the old
In with the new
Big new upgrades coming thru
Don't care no more
For mass recognition
Now I just focus
And honor my mission
Dispelling the spells
And Illusions too
And anything
That isn't true
To my organic
Divine design
I liberate my spirit
Body and mind

GO IN PEACE
by A'Marie B. Thomas-Brown

Not here. Not now. Not ever.

We are waking up to the truth of the who and why we are. It is an embodying that has
carried generations across dunes of sacrifice and resistance since Time memorial that
now calls us to expand into the deepening of That Which Sustains and Supports.

I will not say "don't fall back to sleep," for there is no longer a "back" to go back to
for this reversal is divinely aligning all things to itself.

Divine Remembrance to us all. It is a new day and as the dross of the old fades,
so will the cadence of injustice, inequality and the like.
The shift has happened and our stance reflects Its Glory!

This message may not resonate with all who read it yet it applies nonetheless.
We are One. All is One. We are coming. It is rising. Life goes on.

And so we breathe…

GO IN PEACE

Greater is here.

Transmutation
by Shivrael

I am going to stand with my inner child
as we allow this wave
of ripples in the fabric
of my emotional body to pass.

I AM a soothing presence
to my Self
with the bigger whole of me
connected to Source and eternity.
This is a firefly's flash,
a moment in my life
in which the river of emotion flows.
At this moment I show up
for my younger self
who is crying
and she doesn't know why.

I hold space for her
as the ripple passes through.
A tsunami of emotion
reaches the shores of my being
and I know that we are now
on the other side.

"Feeling is healing"
I remind her, my younger self.
She bravely allows herself
to feel it all
even if she feels scared.
Energy flows again,
and then she is
on the other side.
The witnessing of her feelings
is what is healing her.
She is on the mend,
soon to be laughing.

It makes me smile
to know that my medicine
of pure presence
has done it's magic
and that she and I will be o.k.
once again.

Arrival
by Shivrael

Did you get the message
that the golden age is finally here?
Many are already living this right now!

Are you an early adopter
of the golden age frequency?
Be a beta tester for the new paradigm
in service to all!

Remember to laugh
while trying out the new paradigm.
It is ever-expanding,
endlessly pervading,
and taking over Earth
as the prophecies have foretold.

Look for the signs
and delight
as the waiting is done.

We have arrived.

Sunlight
by Aria Squire

Sunlight thru the window pours
    luminosity ablaze
        lighting my heart
            with unusual desire.
Yet in its strangeness lies a kindred spirit
    the return of the anima
        the wild one
            roaming free
        in nature's home.
    Being true once again
        to the hearts calling
    that knows not of boundaries
    only of indwelling sacred spaces
    fragrant with intoxicating mystery
    beckoning one ever closer still
        inviolate presence.

You Have Other Streams
by Kazi Ayaz Mahesar

And mine are with you
You that hide
And I find you

You, and you think it is I
I your universe
And how you paint me?

Whatever you paint
It is You, it is I

A wing when I fall
Wingless when I fly

A ding in your soul
A soul in my heart

Be Here Now
by Shivrael

It doesn't matter
If today had the strongest solar flares
or if your astrology says
you will have a lousy day.

It matters that
you are here now
in this moment.

That is where the power is-
it is the turning point of
whether you seize the day,
seize the now,
making the best of this life.
Treasure your aliveness,
savor and bask
in your existence

Your presence is a gift.
You are a gift
whether you remember or not.
Everything you experience
is first created from within

You set the tone
that the Universe echoes back.
Moment-to-moment,
Be here now and remember.

Remember who you are
and why you came
which is for the experience of life
and for the Joy of it.

Knickerbocker glory
by Daniel Stone

Borders on
Timeless wonder
Flickered
Rescued
On a sixpence
Returned with love
Like a cat's whisker
Or a Knickerbocker glory
For all to see
With a whiff of cinnamon and
knuckleberry pie
To end all arguments
And start with a moment
Of truth

Being Human
by Cody Ray Richardson

Mind worrier
Addiction conqueror
Possession releaser
Forgiver
Self forgiven
Faith captain
Timeline hopper
Time bender
Now focuser
Acceptor
Moment mentor
Nature student
Psychic
Peace holder
Game piece remover
Puzzle solver
Labyrinth resolver
Metamorphical
Human helper
Light being
Being human

Every Once in a While
by Cheryl

When I write-
it feels like I'm
pouring myself out on paper--
draining my life blood.

Conflict arises within---
my desire to share
and my want
to keep to myself.

Most of the time,
Keep to myself
wins.

But, every once in a while
when the spark shines through--
It is glorious.

Broken Families
by Cheryl

It's wrong
to take a mother's children from her--
whether physically, or
emotionally (by causing conflict).

Who wins?
No one.

Instead try being supportive.

How dare you say
'I can do a better job'!

Instead try being supportive.

Mom, I'm gonna cast a spell to heal
the wound of rejection---
the anger felt and the loss.

You know you didn't do any better.
Why compete with your daughter?

Just be supportive.

Did you know I met my son's father at
the same little bar you took me to as
a young girl?
I used to sit and drink my Coke while playing
songs from the jukebox for a quarter.
It was on Water St. Meadville across
from the market house.
Jerry rented a room upstairs. He'd tie his skinny
black lab to a pole with a rope leash and collar
so he could 'visit' the bar.

What's the saying about the apple
and the tree?

Your not here to see,
But we are doing well.

Accepting each other, child and mother
as we are--
Always
doing our best,
to be supportive.

Healed families.

Rainbow Warrior
by Shivrael

Are you going to wear blinders
to the magnificence unfolding?

Will you keep ignoring seeds of oneness
that are planted everywhere in everyone?

The path forward invites us all
to the Golden Road.

We are the storytellers, truth speakers,
and the creatives
wearing many hats;
wearing costumes of all possible identities
Our message is--
that fear is F.E.A.R.---
False evidence appearing real.

We are the ones we have been waiting for.
The key lies in becoming heart-based.
by feeling the shift
toward more love and light.

Know this:
As inner programs collapse,
the outer reality changes.

You too are a Rainbow Warrior-
Maybe you have yet to claim it?

Let your heart invite you
to our party.
The golden road is paved
with goodness for all.

The new paradigm has landed.

The headline won't be on the news
because we have transcended that to walk
the ancient & modern red road of truth.

Let us restore our Mother Earth
to her primal beauty and
All beings to their divine inheritance.

Your divine inheritance is to
Live and Be in the frequency of Love.

Reflection by Cheryl

In Service to Others
We Step into New Earth--

Thru the mud, snow
and messy trails--

They say no mud
No Lotus.

It may be cold and cloudy,
but the Sun will shine again.

Lily pads are smiling at me--
Golden Rays, rose tipped, streaming.

Under the water--there are layers.

What is under the water?
---We Are---
Come to the surface---

Receive the Sun's blessing.

Freedom
by Cody Ray Richardson

Fantastical freedom to explore
Unleashed from the boundary of the past
Inclusion of all senses
Free from the trouble of who is who
Free from what they will be in our lives
Free from who are we to them
Open to all being a teacher
Unbound by judgment
Hovering at the entrance of consciousness
Like a newborn unable to tell differences
Intelligent before intelligence
Feeling everything
Not far from the veil
A reflection of it still shining through their eyes
Every place is a palace
Everyone is good
Every element gold
Welcome to the now
The only place that ever existed
Can you stand in it
Don't let it drift away like the setting sun
Follow it beyond this moment
Eternal birth
Forever in its womb

To Fly Once More
by Cody Ray Richardson

The bitter end
Is to begin again
On the road
A mind once trapped in a room
Now free to roam
Kicked out is the gift
Termination the ticket
To fly once more
Death is a friend to birth
Though hard to see at the funeral
Ashes are the food
New laughs break patterns of depression
Tears clear the eyes
To see the better path
Ego knows little
Such near vision
The keeper of the now
The bigger picture smiles
The forest laughs at the trees
For it knows
The rest of time
Is the test of time
Hidden treasures await
Pattern in the all
A clefting wave screams
Reaching for the sky
Falling back into its bigger self
Held back by its' why

For the Love of We
by Shivrael

My heart whispered
that it was time for a new direction.

In this game of life

I see a fork:
it is the road not taken,
which is my highest timeline.

Be a pioneer-
blaze the trail

so that others may have an easier
time finding their way.

I do this for the love of We.
I do this because I am called.

How many times have

you ignored your heart's calling
and followed the safer, well-trodden path?

Have you fallen into ruts in life,

running on autopilot
taking the safe route but

missing the grand adventure
of your soul's calling.

Don't miss out.

I Am : We Are
by Cheryl

When you step into the I Am-
you become the great We Are.

It is the great return.
Who else feels it?

It is glorious to live
connected and free---
like the plants and animals,
just doing their thing
not worrying; all in harmony,
naturally,
Not--
Underdressed, Overdressed
Open, Closed----Fitting in?
Wondering...
Do I belong--
SQueezing ourselves into boxes---
Shrinking down so as to please---

Wanting to be a part,
of something, anything--
Not realizing
We Are the Great I Am.

We Stand Out. No longer
able to hide.
We are tall. Towering. Like Tor.*
This is our tower moment.

We will not go quietly. Not silenced--
any more.

We Are.

*Glastonbury Tor

The finite is the moment's gift
by Cody Ray Richardson

Some see the cup half empty
Some see the cup half full
Some see it's both
What do you see
The soul energy
The I AM matter
Two legs to walk
One takes the weight
The other the risk
Two eyes to see
One brain to figure
One mouth to speak
Two ears to listen
The more important being the later
To be born is to die in another life
To learn is to forget something else
To believe is to not learn
To learn is to not believe
You must leave to be
You must be to leave
Forgetting can be the biggest blessing
All the lives you've lived and died
A thousand mistakes
Takes we've tried
All the faces
Infinite spaces
The finite is the moment's gift
If we knew what had been done for us
We would never be depressed
Depression is a disrespect to our ancestors
Yet still authentic
How could we not feel sorrow
Not feel fulfilled
Yet we can turn a knob and get hot clean water
We are richer than kings and queens
If you look forward you are not here
Looking back can wake us
Sometimes the dream seems so real
The pain is meant to keep us here
A friend, a teacher a keeper of the now

Learn from it or not
Keep sleeping or wake
It is here for you
Though hard to see
Don't shoot the messenger

Transformation
by Pradeep Nawarathna

Meditation guides us through life's maze,
Inner transformation sets us free from daze.
Compassion blooms in interdependence true,
Embracing change with a heart anew.

In impermanence, we find our way,
Through mindfulness, clarity each day.
The self is not fixed, but a flow,
Letting go of attachments as they grow.

Coffee
by Dan Crusey

I wanted
To be "spiritual"
To open to the divine

So I got some tattoos
Showed some man cleavage
Did some beach yoga
While hugging a tree
And beating a drum
With a mouthful
Of ayuhuasca
And some crystals
In Bali
Nothing, nada, zip

Then I woke
In my house
Thanked the sun
For coming up
Had some coffee
Reflected on the miracle
Of coffee
Called a songbird brother
And the world
Opened before me

Seeking
by Dan Crusey

You are seeking, seeking
Forever seeking
Panting to see me, touch me
To quench
Your eternal thirst
You could be finding, finding
Forever finding
If you knew not where to look
But how

For I am in that exotic place
And in your own breath
In that transcendent meditation
And in feet on pavement
In the calls of the forest
And a steady fluorescent hum
I am in that yoga class
And the line at the diner
I am the dance of DNA
The shake of a cocktail
The birth of stars
Laughter at sitcoms

For it matters not where you look
But how
And as the man said
Move a stone
And I am there
Cleave wood
And I am there
Let your heart beat
And we are there

The Wheel
by Shivrael

I'm on the cheering squad
Of Babylon falling
As the last of the control system
goes up in smoke.
I see the bigger patterns,
As one age turns into a new one.
Cycles upon cycles,
Ride the wheel
Once again.

Karma comes back again
She can slap you in the face
or bring you to a higher place.

It's based on your consciousness,
It's based on what you put out.
Reality is a mirror
Serving up what you gave to others
upon a silver plate.

We are all shifting together.

Visible, tangible miracles appear
For those with eyes to see.
For some it is invisible-
For others it is coming into form,
The new paradigm arising.

Ride the wheel
Cycles upon cycles,
Ride the wheel
Once again.
let's move into
the Golden Age together.
Let's shift this reality
to a higher place.

The lotus flower blooming
Of all humanity
The oneness era looming

In true unity.
Get on the train
To the highest timeline
And take everyone with you
Who wants to ride the wheel?

Over and over and over again
by Cody Ray Richardson

Over and over and over and over again
Meeting the same soul in a different body
I haven't changed so nothing does
Is it a enemy
Is it a friend
Same situation
Over and over again
They say they want to do shadow work
Then label and push away the supposed red flag
Still putting all the new ones they meet on trial
For unresolved issues with their ex boyfriend and their dad
Cut off one head
Six pop up
Without changing our frequency
It's the same
Over and over and over again
You can change your name
You can change your town
You can change your clothing
There is no hiding
Your mother always knows who and where you are
The path knows you are coming
If thought proceeds matter
Then how are we all actually light
The thought was always the problem
Always will be
Doesn't light matter
What really matters
Can you die again
No rebirth without our it
Can you turn your back on a friend like you should
Or keep enabling yourself through them
You are all that you attract
Over and over and over
High or sober
In a house full of items
On the street full of friends
Can you make the changes
Will you keep playing the game of who is wrong

Who is right
Did anyone one win
When they did, did they get their needs met
Over and over and over again
Keep meeting the same enemy
Keep meeting the same friend
Same soul different body
Same lesson different school
No wrong no right
Are your needs met yet
Are they helping you or are you helping them
Are you hurting you through them
Are they hurting you through themselves
Over and over and over again
Will you walk away
Will you become them
Is it in the answer
Is it in the question
Over and over and over again
The answer is
Stop playing the game
There is no one right
No one wrong
Not you or them to blame
There is no track there is no train
Offer yourself compassion
Offer compassion to them
Burst back into rainbow light
Stop thinking altogether
Just feel
Over and over and over again

Ode to Isis Sophia Maria Magdalena
by Mikasa Tamara Blue Ray

Heaven on Earth, Chalice of Life. The Sacred Womb Portal.
Ode to Isis Sophia Maria Magdalena:

I am Sophia, Divine presence by your birth right.
Anchored deep within your hearts with pure light.

My love guides your path, from wisdom's wellspring, where knowledge flows.
Leading you to cosmic ease from my heart's embrace where a sanctuary bestows.

I am all of the elements, the Ether so clear.
I am the essence that banishes fear.

The Rose's fragrance, a powerful embrace.
Awakens your senses, bringing remembrance of your cosmic trace.

From Pleroma's depths, I fill you with spark.
Igniting creation in flames of the void of dark.

In Oneness with Christ, I reign supreme.
His bride, his luminous, harmonious gleam.

Androgynous Light, Source origin the Song.
I bestow knowledge, truths that belong.

Solomon's wisdom, my domain.
Guiding your soul through life's sacred terrain.

Chalice of Life, I pour out my bliss.
Doves of Peace, I bring solace with each kiss.

Truth I am, righteousness pure and bright.
Strength, hope, and love, your eternal light.

Mary's spirit, Magdalene's embrace, Isis' magic, weaving time and space.
Transforming your dreams with potent wells.

Through challenges, I show the wider view.
Guiding your steps, making your path anew.

Beginning and end, I spiral with Divine time.
Alchemy of Love, a celestial chime.

Storm and calm, I dance upon the waves.
Your humanity and divinity I engrave.

Sophia, your voice, your heartfelt plea.
Healing power of Love, eternally.

Blessed Be!

Dance
by Jennifer Hershelman

When the earth was new
the plants had barely grown
no medicine was known

people needed healing

sisters sat in council
and felt into their hearts
where a primal energy swirled

just as the winds that cross
the plains, bringing in the rain

When they stood together and
stretched their bodies out
the Earth shifted beneath their feet

helping them to feel complete
as they continued stretching
and twirling in the dirt

their hearts overflowed
primal healing rushing
from head to toe

Each movement affecting a change
within the others...
with their hearts beating in harmony
their bodies moving to the rhythm
of their stomping feet, in sync
with the breath of the Earth

The clouds began to swim and shift
with them, the sisters
twist and flow
as rain poured down
the dirt turned to mud

the healing energy,
a giant wave--

Dance as a healing art
was born that day,
a sacred and ancient gift
from the spirits
that is most powerful
when it comes from the heart--
not to be misused to get your way
not to be abused, to lie, cheat and confuse.

It's time.
Come back to the start,
feel it from your heart,
time to hold space for
healing to take place.

Blossoming Time
by Shivrael

When the flower begins to open
I know that I am blossoming
into who I came to be.

When the flower opens
I drink in the sun of my being.
I remember that I am light.
I remember who we are as a people
and why we are here
which is for every being to blossom
into their true full flowering.

My dream is for peace
to rain down upon the planet
like blossom petals in springtime
covering the surface of the ground
with beauty, and then covering
each nation with an aura of peace.

All beings enlightened.
All beings peaceful and free-
that is what we are going for.

All beings express who they are
and why they came here-
with no holds barred,
and nothing held back.

Embodied truth is spoken from every mouth
because the new codes from the sun are here.
The flowering has begun.
The new octave of existence is here.

So let's celebrate as we water the gardens.
Let's give thanks for making it to the flowering stage
with so much beauty,
so much sacredness, and
so much magnificence.
Do not forget that you are this.

When Your Ascending
(Written to the melody *When Your Smiling*)
by Alex Hogstrum

When you're as-cending, when your as-cending the new world opens to you

When you let your loving heart shine you lift up everyone too

But when you're thinking thoughts that are dark

You fall back down and make a world that is stark

So keep as-cending, 'cause when you're as-cending

The whole world as-cends with you

When you rise up to higher dim-ensions you only see what is true

Separation will vanish, leaving only love and me and you

But if you choose to see light and dark

The union you feel will soon fall a-part

So keep as-cending, 'cause when your as-cending,

You bring up everyone with you!

Seraphic Sibyl's Sweven
by Vivian Marie McIntosh

Brothers And Sistars Of Divinity Are Gathering
Together ALL Around The World
Helping Each Other Connect Puzzle Pieces And
Straighten Halos, Wings Growing Unfurled

Ushering Us Back To The Perfect Path Of Psychic
Priests And Priestesses
Pagans Uttering Powerful Prophecies,
Bringing Back Gifts Like Telekinesis

Everyone Won't Believe The Words A Prophet Or
Prophetess Speaks
Truth These Wise Ones Say, Will ALL-Ways Be
Exactly What Our Soul Seeks

Ego, Pride, Fear And Insecurities, Just A Few Of
The Illusions Stunting Our Ra-Membering
Lotsa Issues, Not To Mention Centuries Of
Humans Manifesting Our Own Brainwashing

Ancestors For Too Long Have Given In To Lower
Natures And Floated Along That Frequency
Prohibiting Collective Consciousness Of Humanity
To Activate Dormant DNA, Which Is The Key

ALL Of Creation Is Chosen And Called To Step Up
And Embody Their Higher Self
Go Read Luke 17:21 To Remember Not To Forget,
The Kingdom Of God Is Within Yourself

We Can Never Completely Become The Earth
Angel Of Divinity We Came Here To Be
If We're Not Keeping Our Temple Sacred,
Controlling What We Think, Eat, Speak And See

Keep An Open Mind Long Enough For The Truth Of
His-Story To Find And Fill Your Brain
Developing A Pure Heart And Cherishing Crystal
Clear Intentions, Is How You'll Attain

Universal Knowledge, Telepathy, Clairvoyance, And
So Many More Godly Gifts Will Be Granted
Let Go Of Judgmental Thoughts That Only Fuel Division,
It's ALL Programmed And Implanted

Living And Speaking Truth Even When it's Not Easy
Or Accepted As The Popular Opinion
Breaking Free From Ancestral Karma And Stop
Looping And Being A Matrix Minion

ALL-Ways Doing the Right thing, As Well As
Keeping Your Heart As Light As A Feather
Warm Welcome Wishes To Angels With Green Lips
Who Glow Golden When Under Pressure

We're Living In The Age Of Aquarius, No Deceit
Or Duality, Only A United As One Miracle
The Days Of The Aquarian Heralds, Whom Walk
And Talk In Truth To Transform Into An Oracle

Luke 17:21 (KJV)
*"Neither shall they say, Lo here! or, lo there! For, behold,
the kingdom of God is within you."*

The Regreening
by Sabina and Herd of Light

The Regreening
of your inner world
is the most important work
you have
in the world,
for the world,
at this time.

What is this Regreening?
A return to your innate,
natural innocence.
A return to the newborn nature
of your
    True Being.
And where is this newborn, where can this newborn be witnessed,
nourished and given
all one's heart to?

Here. Now.

In the all-pervading, replenishing womb of Silence
    surrounding all.
Feel the unclenching from fear as Silence re-supples your whole
Being.
Inner clenching transforms into open handed mudra,
circulating,
giving back to
and receiving
from the whole universe
    as One Flow.

Here,
feel the complex webs of doubt release,
complexity simplifies and purifies
and your once parched, shallow roots extend into the depths
of the Silent Ground of
Here and Now,
deepening their limitless reach
into the fertile soul soil
    of Faith.

Faith in the newborn who inherently knows how to grow,
like flower in the sun,
freed from complexity
of mind mapping out the way.

Now,
mind breathes its own
newborn nature,
sensing the simplicity of the Way
as the very doorway
of
    Here and Now.

Mosaic of Light
by Mikasa Tamara Blue Ray

Shattered patterns, like glass on the ground.
Huge collective release.
Bringing much needed peace.
Glass on the ground, a mosaic of light.
Reflecting a future, hopeful and bright. Grace.
New path unfolding, in our collective space.

What' ya Gonna Do about It
by Cody Ray Richardson

Against the grain
Undeserving pain
In a world of crazy people
Feeling insane
Why wonder
You know who you are
Perplexed as to why
Things are the way they are
Characters with no character
The pendulum swings
Don't become what they are
There are no enemies
There is no right or wrong
Only needs met or unmet
Strange how some go about it
With ill intent
Karma is a boomerang
What you throw comes back
It's hard with the safety delay
To give and give in time of lack
It takes time to prime the pump
We see our old selves in others
In others action is the grandmother
In a hall of mirrors
All is a reflection
Don't get caught up in this closed loop system
Acting with ill intentions
Be who you are
As you would want them to be
Sit back and watch it grow
Your actions are your seeds
Tend to the garden
Don't go chasing bugs
They are who they are
All is love

Hour Glass
by Cody Ray Richardson

It makes no difference
if it's the first or last grain of sand in the hour glass that drops
If unbroken all has its date
No one grain is more significant than the other at the time
Oh how twisted it is to borrow sand from other hour glasses
Breaking the glass in the process
Yet it is the way of this world
This world only being one world
To borrow from other hour glasses is to stay in the way of this world
Letting the sand fall naturally
is to know we are neither the sand nor the hour glass
This is to know the knowing of eternal life

Are we the sand, or the hourglass?

Mabe we are neither.
Like grains of sand,
we are...
being washed away,
back and forth.

 Like snowflakes clustered
on the tree branch,
Are we more when we are together?

Look away, to see
look away
(Awaaaaaay)

----Cheryl

KALEIDOSCOPE
by Tommy Allen

Ever changing
the world we know
always evolving
as we tune in the show

the kaleidoscope of life
right in your eyes
tuning out those
who only tell lies

this circle of life
we now go thru
stepping on stones
and other things we do

the turning scope
first offers you red
bringing to life
the things in your head

the turning scope
orange as you see
fear is the lock
your heart is the key

the turning scope
now turns to blue
& more wonderful things
come out of you

the turning scope
now yellow so bright
filling your heart
as day turns to night

the turning scope
suddenly turns black
exposing your fears
and all that you lack

empty inside
it just isn't fair
a turning scope
colors everywhere

with each offering yet
a different view
of what's always been
deep Inside of you

Starfish Message by Dave Harvey

Every moment is a gift, every emotion a miracle.
You are free to assimilate this, or ignore, anyway you prefer.
Obviously there are unwanted moments and emotions that can curl your teeth.
That's what drives creation.
That's what expands the universe.
That's what keeps you coming back.
You don't have to remember who you really are, but you're going to.
-Starfish

You are: Intuitive, Resilient, Sovereign

Goat's Message by Dave Harvey

Anger is fear, depression is fear, anxiety is fear.
Fear has been part of our survival for so long we find comfort in it.

There are legitimate things to fear in this environment and there are fears we cling to unnecessarily.

Your job, my brothers and sisters, is to weed out the concerns that are meaningless.

Once a fear has been shown to be a crutch, it disappears. This is commonly referred to as letting go of that which no longer serves.

How to do that is the mystery only self love can solve.

Relax.
Your potential is greater than your ability to understand.
-Goat

Permission
by Mikasa Tamara Blue Ray

Heaven on Earth,
26-02-2025, 65, 11, 2 + 2222 = 22222!
The key with a code: 22222. 10. One. Zero. New beginnings.
A letting go and a letting in.

February 26th, 2025... 26-02-2025... 6+5=11, 1+1=2... 22222.
The golden key with a code. Opening the door, a swirling vortex of Divine Feminine energy. Intuition. Balance. Harmony. Trust. Cooperation.

Ascending with Mother Earth. Revealing a sun-drenched landscape behind the unlocked door. A feeling of lightness and clarity.

This isn't just numerology; it's permission. Give yourself Permission to trust your gut, to follow that voice of your intuition, to make choices aligned with your heart.

The Frequency of 22222 is about aligning.
Like tuning a finely crafted instrument,
finding that perfect resonance.

It's the frequency of release. It's about releasing the energy blocks, the things that holds you back. Unblocking your flow.
It's about faith, about trusting that the universe, your higher self, has your back.
That guidance is there, present in the spaces between the numbers.

New beginnings. That's what it is. Not some dramatic upheaval, but a quiet shift, a subtle realignment. A letting go and a letting in.

It's about trusting yourself, daring to believe in the possibilities that lie ahead. Finally listening to and enjoying the breathtaking melody your heart is playing.

The 22222 Frequency announces that good things have come. You have invited them in through using your golden key to unlock that door. All you need to do now is trust, listen, and dare to play your song.

Hunters
by Benjamin Prasad

What if ideas were hunters?
That they tracked us down,
From some misty dimension
Out of space and time,
Seeking to manifest through our neurology

And they took aim, praying,
'Just sit still.
I'm coming.
I'm the answer.
Don't struggle.'

What if Nature is intelligent
And we just have to stop trying,
Stop doing everything
That God intended to do for us?
Looking

With scarce eyes clawing
Through the Root Cellar seeking,
For a plump idea, not too moldy,
To Nourish our belief,
That we are the Gardener?

When these words seeped
out of the spring of the Unmanifest
to trickle across this page,
I realized,
I am just a thirsty animal.

When these ideas cracked through concrete
and sprouted a whole landscape
of medicinal herbage
I didn't hesitate
To fatten myself.

And had I ever needed to spend time
In the dark cellar seeking?
Wondering
What that smell is, And what I stepped in?

Now I feast in the Open Field
My teeth green
my hands cupped, gathering Water
And the hunter's crosshairs
Tickle my neck,

Whispering
'Just sit still.
I'm coming.
I'm the answer.
Don't struggle.'

Personality
by Benjamin Prasad

I tried to kiss
the Great I AM
's ass...

Wasn't it a lie?
Me, feigning dispassion,
Imitating my hero, Space?

I can't wear my crown,
Because you'll see I still have a head.
Gotta avoid those crosshairs.

Flat faced, I was really just afraid.
Remember what happened last time?
God's personality got him killed.

That terrible wedding
Was saved.
The Son put a ring around the entire Earth.

The arms of the Cross
Extend the whole horizon
Right clasps left.

Moves like that
take personality.

Worthy
by Jennifer Hershelman

People lost, thinking
worthiness is something that has to be attained
to be gained

Rolling on the ground thinking
they have to be trained

-Fetch, Go get it
get the stick
get the job
get the money
get the car

Do it now. Do it right. Bring it back.
Prove your worth.

-people lost, believing the lie
Well, its time to be found
let the lie fall to the ground

You are worthy
by your very presence
your soul, your every essence
is essential and enough

It's time to let go
No more hoops
No more lies
See with unclouded eyes

You are worthy just by being
So, thank you for being

Standing in my Sovereignty
by Jennifer Hershelman

Writing in a dream,
phantoms of my true authentic self
watching me from shards of broken glass-

The promised Avalon waiting for me,
All eyes on me, will I fulfill the prophesy?

What am I willing to sacrifice
when knights of darkness come at me
with sword and staff, will I bend, or break.

What am I willing to allow them to take?
Nothing!

Standing in my Sovereignty.

Dancing the ancient Dance of Power
letting them know they can't keep me
locked in their tower.

Guinevere, Merlin & Morgan La Fey
all hold council.

Watching the storm unfold
as I alchemize the facade fades.

Heart Beat True
by Pradeep Nawarathna

The clock ticks on, so let it be,
Past worries and future fears set free.
Take a breath, feel your heart beat true,
This moment now is all that's due.
The weight you carry, gently release,
In simple presence, find your peace.
One life to live beneath the sun,
Make each breath count until you're done.

Perfectly Imperfect Art
by Pradeep Nawarathna

Hold your own hand when the path gets tough,
Love yourself first when days feel rough.
Your journey is yours, no need to compare,
Take one small step, breathe in fresh air.
Dreams need tending, like seeds that you sow,
Give yourself time and space to grow.
One life, one heart—perfectly imperfect art,
Be gentle, be patient, love who you are.

We Are Returning
by Rune Darling

1.

Darkness Fell Upon Us
But Under The Vernal Equinox

.

When The Tree Of Life Is Crowned
When Birch Is Dressed In Black & White

.

The Sagittarius Shall Call The Moon
In The Blue & Green Veil Of The Night

.

Shadows Of The Celtic Trees Disappear
And Now We Are Returning Back Again

.

We Carry No Shadows Only Light &
Tie Ribbons In Springtime Of This Now

.

Songs Of Bluebirds Will Float Our Planet
And All Our Voices Shall Be Heard

2.

Darkness Fell Upon Us
But Under The Vernal Equinox
.

When The Cosmic Doula Is Crowned
When Scorpio Calls In The Gentle Seas
When Father Dissolves The Opium Sky
When Birch Balance Black & White
.

Healing The Shadows Of Women & Men
Now We Are Returning Back Again
We Carry Our Shadows In Light
Evolving DNA Is In All Of Our Might
.

Songs Of Bluebirds Will Float Our Planet
And All Our Voices Shall Be Heard
Joined Together We Link Our Hands
Round In Circles And In Æon Flux
.

So The Journey Of The Souls Descend
When All The Shadows Are Grey
At Our Door - The Portal We Stand
The Work Of Our Own Hands
.

Now Returning Back Again
We Bring A New Day

The End Game
by Rune Darling

In This World
Dimensional Doors
Are Frequencies
.
In The Power Of Now
We Enter The Doors Between
We Are Entering The End Game
.
Surrendering It All Is Key
Breaking Bad Habits
Of An Unbalanced Ego
.
Cracked Open The Eggs
Birthing The Divine
Feminine & Masculine
.
As We Run Out Of Time
Christ Consciousness
Is Upon Us For Evermore
.
Delivering Hope
In The Quantum Field
In A Heart Beat

Many thanks to these contributors:

Tommy Allen
A'Marie B. Thomas-Brown
Dan Crusey
Rune Darling
Dave Harvey
Jennifer Hershelman
Alex Hogstrum
Kazi Ayaz Mahesar
Vivian Marie McIntosh
Pradeep Nawarathna (pcnawarathna@gmail.com)
Zin Onyx
Benjamin Prasad
Mikasa Tamara Blue Ray
Cody Ray Richardson
Sabina and Herd of Light
Shivrael
Daniel Stone
Aria Squire
Mercy Talley
Danielle Turner

Author page--

Cheryl Lunar Wind lives in the Mount Shasta area in a little town called Weed. She is a practicer of Mayan cosmology, Lakota ceremony, Star Knowledge and theUniversal Laws including the Law of One. Her hobbies are writing poetry, music, dance, drum circles and love for all life; plant, animal and crystal. Cheryl has been a guide and spiritual teacher for many years. Now she shares wit and wisdom through poetry, and has published poetry books; Know Your Way, We Are One, Follow the White Rabbit,
Love Your Light, LIFE: Shared thru Poetry, Come to Mount Shasta: Sacred Path Poetry, We Are Light, Finding Our Way Home, We Are Forever, Handshake With the Divine,
Grand Rising: A New Day Has Dawned, Star Messages: Codes to Sing, Dance and Live by, Return to Innocence, Bloom Like Nature: Live the Natural Way, Creativity Brings Peace: Create & Share Your Gifts, May Love Lead: Poetry for Living, Loving & Giving, The Eventful Flash: Bringing Solar Waves of Change, The Setting Sun, Crossroads of Change and now Step Into New Earth.

Testimonials---

"Cheryl's poetry is very inspiring--particularly the way she compares life with the forces of nature. There is a special element in her poems that opens my heart and fills my soul with divine possiblities."
Giovanna Taormina, Co-Founder, One Circle Foundation

"Cheryl's poems have helped me to uncover and honor my own hidden memories. The beauty of her spirit is evident in each tender, insightful passage."
Marguerite Lorimer, www.earthalive.com

"A rare collection filled with raw, courageous honesty. Thought provoking words that will stop you in your tracks."
Snow Thorner, ED Open Sky Gallery, Montague, California

"When wisdom, guidance, confirming comfort, ect. arrives to us humans--from beings with the perspective of other realms--it is a divine gift. Especially in the form of what we call poetry, and through a being with no agenda; Cheryl Lunar Wind simply shares what source gives her!"---Dragon Love (Thomas) Budde

Made in the USA
Monee, IL
30 March 2025